"Do They Celebrate Christmas In Heaven?"

Spiritual
Rite of Passage Teachings
From Children
with Life-Threatening
Illness

———

THOMAS SOLOWAY PINKSON, PH.D.

ISBN 0-9647542-3-1

Printed in USA by 48HrBooks (www.48HrBooks.com)

Originally published by:
Wakan Press
P.O. Box 788
Woodacre, CA 94973

Cover photograph by Andrea Danek Pinkson.
Designed by Michael Saint James.

This publication was made possible by the generous donation of Bobby Sarnoff. Thank you so much.

*THE JOURNEY
OF LIFE AND DEATH
IS A SACRED
CIRCLE.*

*WITHIN
ITS CENTER
LIES THE GIFT OF
PEACE.*

INTRODUCTION

In 1977 I joined forces with Dr. Jerry Jampolsky in working with children with life-threatening illness at the Center for Attitudinal Healing in Tiburon, California.

The center was a new program in its beginning stages and Jerry asked me to join him in a group with youngsters using principles he had drawn from the *Course of Miracles.*

The course teaches about the healing presence of love which can he accessed by learning to use our conscious minds to choose peace over pain, and love over fear.

More easier said than done, as we all know from our own life experience.

Nevertheless, the intention of the initial children's group was to provide a safe and supportive setting where the adult facilitators would attempt to he non-judgmental and unconditionally loving thereby allowing all group participants, adults included, to explore their thoughts and feelings about illness, treatment, death, loss and whatever else was going on in their lives. Another intention was to nurture the growth of peer support based on the idea that people going through similar experiences could reach out to one another with a legitimacy that could forge deep and meaningful connections.

This is in fact exactly what happened. At the end of the six-week group, the children all wanted to keep going and from that humble start, Centers for Attitudinal grew up around the world, offering groups of peer support for children, families and adults facing life threatening illness, as well as support groups for those without illness who seek to learn and apply the principles of attitudinal healing in their personal lives, at home, at work and in their communities.

Prior to entering the group for the first time I was very anxious about what would happen, what could I do to be of help, and how would I hold up under the pressure of dealing with children suffering under such frightful conditions of cancer itself, as well as the invasive treatment methodologies that were a vital part of their young lives. I will always remember Jerry's words to me just before going in to the room. "Just love them Tom, that's all you have to do."

"Yeah, sure," I thought to myself. "Easy for him to say, but it sounds so simplistic and naive. There has to he more to it than that," I mused fearfully to myself. Then I walked into the room, entering a doorway much bigger than the wooden frame my physical body passed through. I entered a room of wisdom teachers in little, frail and sometimes deformed bodies. I walked into a room of BIG spirits, whose courage, grace under pressure, compassion, humor, valor and love was enormous. They became my teachers in learning how to open my heart to a healing power and presence that was immense. They taught me that this power existed for one purpose and one purpose only-for giving. They showed me that love truly was for giving and doing so with out any conditions, strings, or attachments. They demonstrated time and again that giving hearts could join together to create the deepest healing-the healing of inner peace and knowing the presence of love.

"Do They Celebrate Christmas in Heaven?" is about these young teachers as they face life's final rite of passage, the passage into death. Like shooting stars blazing across the sky, shining so brightly but lasting for such a short time, the spirits of these wisdom elders in young bodies did not live long on this earth plane. But in their passing they left teachings that hold up even stronger and stronger as the years of my own life move ever onward.

Death is the great equalizer, it comes for us all, some sooner, some later, but no one escapes its ultimate call.

In a materialistic culture that spends billions of dollars annually to convince us that the purpose of life is buying, consuming and accumulating things, the sacraments of birth, death, sexuality and living integral lives of service to humanity and the natural world all get short thrift.

These children and their spiritual teachings bring death out of the closet and confront us with looking at how we live our lives, what is most important about living a good life and finally, how we face the end of the life we have known when death comes calling at our door.

In my thirty years of journeying around the world to study with indigenous peoples who still follow the ways of their ancestors, I notice that death and dying is part and parcel of their daily lives. Shamanic cultures take their young people through rites of passage, such as the solitary vision quest in a wilderness setting that expose the participant to death and the mysteries beyond. This empowers the kind of healthy respect for life and the gifts each person carries that we see too little of in our more technologically advanced societies.

We have much to learn from these cultures, as we do from the children in *"Do They Celebrate Christmas in Heaven?"*. They both have penetrated a system of denial to see more clearly the truths of what is most important during our stay here on Planet Earth.

I invite you to join with the still living spirit of my young teachers from the Center as they help you explore your own life and death to come. They teach the age-old wisdom of love, now, today. Up to the last lit breath. And on in to the Great Mystery.

" Tom Pinkson's sensitive and deep teachings from the heart with children allows us to have another way of looking at life and death."
Gerald G. Jampolsky, M.D.
Author of *Love is Letting Go of Fear*

"Read his work as you would the instructions to the Elixer of Life."
Stephen Levine
Author of *Who Dies?*

A PERSONAL ASSIGNMENT

Bryan was eight years old and bedridden with cancer. He'd been fighting a hard battle that included an amputation of one leg from the hip down, several lung surgeries, and intensive sessions of chemotherapy and radiation. Still the cancer had spread throughout his body.

There was nothing else that could he done medically and Bryan's parents brought him home to die. I met Bryan through his involvement in the Children's Group of the Center for Attitudinal Healing in Sausalito California, where I serve as a clinical consultant. Over the years I had frequently visited him at home and during his numerous hospital stays. It looked like this might be our last visit.

Bryan's mother told me he was upstairs and probably wouldn't talk much because of the sedative effect of the pain-killing drugs he was taking. I went upstairs to his room. Bryan was lying very still with his eyes closed. The nearby TV was blasting away. I sat down next to his bed and greeted him. Several minutes went by as I sat in silence watching his indomitable spirit struggle for breath in his pain-wracked body. Then Bryan opened his eyes and sat up. He could barely muster enough strength to set up his pillow to support an upright position. I leaned over to help him get comfortable.

He looked at me, suddenly clear-eyed and earnest, and asked, "Do They Celebrate Christmas in Heaven?"

"And, what about Easter, do they celebrate that too? Will there be a house for me like my house here?"

I was struck dumb by the suddenness and impact of his questions. My mind raced inward for answers, but there were none to he found.

"What's it like to die?" he asked. "Does it hurt?"

It was six weeks before Christmas and Bryan knew he probably wouldn't make it to this important holiday. He'd miss celebrating it with his family as he had done all of his young life up to now. What was to come for this valiant little fighter soon to die?

Bryan was one of many important teachers for me over the past fifteen years of working with people facing life threatening illness. His blunt, heartfelt questions triggered a powerful confrontation within my psyche, similar to previous ones experienced with other children and adults on their passage into death. These confrontations have enriched my life immeasurably through the lessons they have provided.

This book fulfills an "assignment" to extend these lessons to others, as I know they were given not just for me alone. The concept of assignment-fulfillment comes from a fourteen-year old boy as he lay in bed two days before his death from Ewing's Sarcoma.

"Everybody has an assignment in life," he told me. "That's why we're here, to work on it. Sometimes they're longer and sometimes they're shorter, like with me," he added. But that's why we're here, to work on our assignment. And when we're finished, we get to graduate."

The experience of graduation, or death, is one transitional passage we all must face. It is the great equalizer. Unlike other times of transition in the life cycle which might be ignored, repressed or unacknowledged, death demands our attention.

I was painfully introduced to this fact at the age of four when my father died. Years later, while finishing my doctoral work in psychology, I received a suggestion that led me into the field of thanatology professionally, in addition to my personal involvement. I asked a member of my doctoral committee, Dr. William Lamers, what kind of client population he thought I would be most effective working with. I was shocked at his response:

"People that are dying," he said. "People that are dying are on a Vision Quest. They may not articulate it that way, but they are. You've been taking people out for years now, guiding them on vision quests and this is what you could do for the dying.

The Vision Quest is a rite of passage into spiritual adulthood practiced by numerous Native American tribes in which a questing youth enters the wilderness for a period of isolation and solitude, to seek guidance from the Great Spirit for their life path.

In my book, *A Quest for Vision*, I describe utilizing the vision quest as a model for a successful substance-abuse program I developed in 1972. Both the original vision quest, as well the facsimile I developed, included dynamics inherent in all traditional rites of passage. These are severance, or letting go; transition/transformation; and return or incorporation. Rites of passage, as psychologist Dr. Jean Houston notes, are "doors through which one passes into larger life." They provide a form and support structure for powerful psychological processes during times of transition that, left unchanneled, might otherwise prove overwhelming to the psyche. The rituals and ceremonies of effective rites of passage supply a secure, protected space where strong emotions can he openly experienced, thereby leading to transformation into new identity and developmental stages of growth. Successful ritual frees the conscious mind through its direction of all necessary functions involved with the occasion. Participants are thereby able to surrender into the full psychological/emotional dimensions of the experience which includes, via the ritual, a joining of the personal with the collective, the inner with the outer, and the unconscious with the conscious.

Essential to all rites of passage is symbolic death and rebirth. The movement into and birth of the new, cannot take place without the release, or death, of the old. Severing the security of the known, such as leaving the comforts and safety of home to enter the darkness of the unknown in the wilderness, as one does on a Vision Quest, dramatically elicits these dynamics. Rebirth is the return and incorporation back into the social collective with a new identity based on the quest outing. When I reflected on the quest dynamics and the process of dying, I saw that Bill Lamers' assessment of their similarity was correct. When he asked me several months later to join with him and a team of others in starting the second Hospice program in the United States, I accepted the invitation.

My experience with Hospice patients evidenced a paucity of effective psychosocial/emotional and spiritual support systems for the dying and their families, especially when they were not practicing members of a specific faith.

Another observation was the significant role the patient's belief system and attitudinal mindset played in effecting the quality of their experience during their final stage of life.

Virginia Hine, anthropologist and author of *Last Letter to the Pebble People*, describing her husband's death from cancer and its effect on family members, comments on the importance of these factors. She feels death forces us beyond the rational mind into a confrontation with spiritual reality. How we handle this confrontation helps determine whether "death is dehumanizing or transforming."

"What we bring," states Hine, "can enhance or detract from death's power to transform and spiritualize."

"It is quite possible," she goes on, "that a gradual spiritualization of consciousness is what life is all about." The altered states of her husband, described in her book, as well as many I witnessed through my Hospice work, did indeed appear to he an acceleration of the "spiritualization of consciousness" process that she suggests.

I left Hospice after a year to focus on working with children facing life threatening illness at the Center for Attitudinal Healing in Sausalito, California. The Center was just getting started and to my excitement embodied a philosophy that recognized and validated the spiritual dimension of being.

My learning process intensified at the Center. One outgrowth has been a reevaluation and subsequent transformation of my "death myth." A death myth is the totality of our conscious and unconscious beliefs and assumptions on the meaning of death and what happens afterwards. The dominant Western cultural death myth focuses on the negative. It is an outgrowth of the "single order of reality, master-myth" that posits the material, physical world as all there is. In other words, if we can't see, or measure or quantify it in some way, it does not exist. In such a materialistic perspective, there is little, if any, room for notions of soul, spirit or any quality of being transcendent of the physical. We have lost touch with the numinous ground of our deeper being that is something more than the sum of the physical properties of the body. Sitting next to a lifeless body forcefully brings this into awareness. The physical body lies there before you, completely intact, with all its parts and components still there. But something has gone out of that body which was the real essence of the person. What remains is an empty shell. Yet that essence quality of life- force cannot be measured under a microscope or weighed on a scale.

In the dominant cultural death myth, death is seen as an enemy coming to get you; the Grim Reaper. Bryan's bedside questions opened a door to explore our mutual death myths. A "prime function of mythology and rite," states Joseph Campbell, "is to supply the symbols that carry the human spirit onward,"

13

and the "common denominator of all mythic systems is their meaning-provoking capacity."

Looking into the face of his own oncoming death, Bryan reached out for meaning and symbols to carry his spirit onward.

I had no definite answers for Bryan.

Truth was all I could give him now. I told him I didn't know if they celebrated Christmas in Heaven. Then, without thinking, I said, "But if they do and you find out before me, let me know and I'll tell the other kids at the Center." Bryan nodded his head in agreement. We then went on to share our fears and anxieties about dying. We shared our hopes and fantasies of who we'd like to have welcome us on the "other side," should that turn out to be what happens.

I felt total joining and equality with Bryan, even with our thirty years age differential, because in the areas we covered, there are no real answers, only our own thoughts and feelings which we shared freely without fear of judgment or pressure to believe in someone else's program.

Bryan thought that when we die, we go to heaven, and get to make a choice whether to stay there, or return to earth as a helper for someone else.

"I think I'd choose to stay," I told him, "What about you?"

Bryan thought long and hard, his face grimacing in concentration. "I don't know. I guess I'll just have to decide when I get there," he replied.

I told Bryan of children I'd seen die and that the actual process of dying didn't appear to he painful. Perhaps there had been pain previously, as with Bryan himself, but the act of life leaving the body seemed to be very peaceful from what I had seen. Bryan had more questions and feelings to explore and we went on until suddenly he paused, sat up from his pillow enthusiastically,

"I feel better!" His face lit up in a big smile.

"I do too," I answered, and we gave each other a big hug. I knew my work with Bryan was finished and we said our good-byes. Then I went downstairs to see his mother and younger sister who also needed time to express their feelings.

The next day Bryan's mother called the Center to report that Bryan had just died. He answered his own question about the painfulness of death by dying very peacefully.

He had just finished a relaxing warm bath and was lying in bed with both parents present.

I thought back to my conversation with him the day before and reflected on Bryan's "teaching lessons," I saw that more important than what actually happened after death, was what the person believed happened. The belief held in the moment was the causative factor in determining the person's immediate experience. It was a parallel teaching with the Buddhist notion that the mind state creates one's phenomenological world. Bryan was showing me the power of the focused mind in helping to realize a death with dignity.

He also showed me the importance of allowing the dying person to explore their mind-state in a non-judgmental setting, devoid of pressure to believe in any particular ideology. Bryan spoke freely of his fears and anxieties, his hopes and wishes regarding his death. He was thus able to release his fears, and, as he put it, "feel better." He achieved a state of inner peace that accompanied him into and through his lying. My part in being with him was to he fully open and present in the moment, to not impose anything or expect or want anything and to extend unconditional love. Bryan was thus free to address his fears. He didn't have to take care of me, or fear judgment or pressure to change. Instead of feeling separate and alone, he experienced joining through love which brought peace us both.

Through our sharing Bryan actualized his own symbols and myth to "carry his spirit onward" into his peaceful death.

OLD PROPHETS IN YOUNG BODIES

Another powerful teacher was Erik, a ten year old friend of Bryan's and mine from the Children's Group at the Center who had leukemia.

Erik was angry and in pain when his mother asked me to visit him at home. Six weeks earlier Erik and I had traveled together to Oregon to address a conference on attitudinal healing. Erik's illness had just reoccurred and he knew that without a miracle, his chances of living much longer were very slim.

"Why does this happen to me?" he asked. Half of my life I've been sick with leukemia. Just when I start getting better, I get sick again. It's not fair."

He admitted he was angry at God. He also felt guilty for this and had been keeping it inside, adding more stress to his pained body. I suggested it was okay to he angry with God and to let it come out, that God didn't need our protection. Erik thought for a while, then agreed and was able to talk out his anger and frustration.

We then did some relaxation and guided imagery to lessen his pain (using imagination to see the pain as sharp, hot swords sticking him which he then proceeded to visualize himself pulling out and releasing with his out-breath. Then with the in-breath he visualized a soothing presence bathing the wounds in a healing light). After these exercises Erik continued with his questions.

"Why is this happening to me?" he pleaded.

17

"I don't know why, Erik, and I wish it weren't happening to you or anyone else.

"But what I do know is that when you ask the 'why' questions, I notice your pain gets worse again."

He nodded in agreement with my observation.

"It does look like death is coming closer, but it's not here now, and right now is all we've got," I reminded us both.

"What do you want to have now Erik?" I asked, Peace or pain.

"I want peace," he said with conviction,

"Then we need to stop asking the 'why' questions," I stated.

The next step was over an immense cavern of darkness that, when taken successfully, brings liberation. I knew from previous conversations that Erik believed in a reality beyond the material world. He had talked about ESP experiences we'd both had and our belief in mystery underlying the observable world of physical phenomena. I reminded Erik of our mutual belief that there was more going on here than what we could see with our eyes or know with our minds:

"Some how, in some way, if we can open up to having trust and faith that through all this terrible stuff that's happening, in a way we can't see or understand and that we don't have to like, but still it's happening, that something is working for the good. Maybe it can help us feel peaceful.

Now this is a great deal to ask of anyone, least of all a ten-year old boy dying of cancer who hasn't had a chance to do half of what he'd dreamed of doing with his life. I reminded Erik that he did have the power to choose what he put his attention into and that this choice would determine his experience in the moment. Erik was silent for several minutes. Then he looked directly at me and sat up on his bed. I remembered times at the Center when we'd start the Children's Group by all of us holding hands in a circle and sending love to each other and to those of our group who weren't there with us that night. Without speaking, we both reached out and took each other's hands. Our eyes closed, I suggested that we send our love to his parents and younger brother in the adjoining room. We focused on our own hearts opening and a beam of love flowing into Erik's family. I didn't know how many minutes passed because all measurement of time stopped. I experienced a feeling of unification with Erik, myself, his parents and his brother. When we opened our eyes Erik was pain-free and ready to see his family. I left shortly afterwards, bringing his peacefulness with me.

Erik's mother called several days later to report that Erik had died. She asked if I would speak at his memorial service and then spoke of a great gift Erik had given then in the last days of his life.

"Erik brought God's presence into our home," she said, "It was so filled with peace, so special," she added, a blessing that helped them release Erik into his peaceful passage.

Erik and Bryan each demonstrated the power of inner peace to transform an otherwise tragic situation into a sacred opportunity for spiritual joining.

There is indeed more going on than meets the eye.

HUMANIZING DEATH

A seventeen year old girl with cystic fibrosis, Mary Beth, shared with me a discovery that transformed her last few days on earth as well. She had prayed as a little girl for God to take away her fatal illness. When he didn't, she stopped believing in Him.

During her last hospitalization before coming home to die, she reopened the relationship and had a conversation with God,

"I realized," she said, that God isn't necessarily a force that will take things away that you don't like. But He'll he there with you," she added, "as you go through them."

Mary Beth, Bryan and Erik are teachers for the rest of us on the importance of trust in the letting go process. Life itself, as well as the final passage of life into the mystery of what we call death, is an ongoing flow of cyclic change. From the level of the micro to the level of macro, the old must he released before the new can he horn. The old breath must leave our body to enable the new one to enter. Rites of passage, such as the vision quest, were vehicles of experience in aboriginal cultures that supported and empowered the release of the old and the birth of the new. They offered a little death, which in turn helped prepare participants for the bigger death awaiting them when their "assignments" were completed. Repeated involvement in rites of passage throughout the life cycle helped strengthen trust and confidence on surrendering ego control into the mysterious unknown. Successful outcome of previous release into the unknown via rites of passage, gave participants psycho-spiritual strength and confidence with which

20

to face their physical death with faith in another positive outcome. They were able to die with dignity, a humanizing death, as did Erik, Bryan and Mary Beth.

At the time of death there is a vital need for a death myth that empowers a passage of dignity. A death myth emerging from the experiences with these children suggests that death is something we do, it doesn't just happen to us. Just as Dr. Frederick LeBoyer introduced more loving process into the labor and delivery of newborns, so are Bryan, Erik and others like them, helping us to see that physical death is a birthing as well. It is a birthing back into spirit that also deserves a loving process. "The body is a placenta to the soul," states philosopher/anthropologist Terence McKenna.

I see now that my work with Bryan and Erik was analogous to that of a labor coach with a woman giving birth to a baby. The birth process associated with death of the physical body, the "placenta", is of the soul back into union with the ongoing flow of the cosmos. From this perspective, the deterioration of left-brain faculties, that frequently occur during the dying process confused and impaired logical and linear thought, may warrant new evaluation. Rather than merely pathological disorganization and hallucination, it may indicate a shift from the rational mode into a visionary state usually associated with right-brain function. As such, it offers opportunity for exploration and growth for the dying person that merits our support and reassurance.

The "doing" of letting go is integral to this birthing with dignity, just as it is with the letting go into labor contractions that

21

push the infant out into the physical world. Barbara, who was 36 years old when she died of metastasis from breast cancer, taught me a great deal about this kind of "doing." She had also undergone lengthy and painful bouts with surgery, radiation and chemotherapy. Barbara was ready to die when I visited her at her apartment. She had suffered long enough, had said goodbye to her family and loved ones, and now wanted to be alone as she waited for death. Barbara had her own vision of what death would he like, and she felt ready to meet it through her preparation work of mediation and prayer. The only problem was that death didn't come when she wanted it to.

For days she waited in her darkened bedroom, growing increasingly impatient and frustrated. Her faith in what death would he like began to crumble. When I saw her she was cursing and yelling, interspersed with violent coughing fits, for death to finally take her.

Angry and defiant, she didn't understand why this was happening to her when she was so ready and well prepared. Sitting down next to her on the bed, I sat silent while she continued her bursts of anger. Her strength was ebbing, but her suffering was not. As Barbara and I looked at her experience, we gradually saw that she was still holding on to her expectation of how death would he for her. Her anger was itself a holding on. We saw together that she needed to let her expectations die. Each shallow breath brought in something new.

"Open to its presence," I urged her.

"Follow it to wherever it takes you. Release expectations as

22

you breath out.

"Let them go. Let them die. Open to the new while releasing the old. Let the old breath die until your last release gently carries you on," I whispered.

Barbara was calm now, and I took my leave. She died several hours later. Her death taught me that in the process of dying, our preconceptions can he excess baggage which interfere with the impending journey. They too, must he allowed to die for the greater birth to occur.

Another teaching of the "doing" of letting go into death, involved a family and their doctor, who had become close friends through his loving care of their thirteen-year old son, Adrian. I knew Adrian from the Children's Group at the Center. His family called when Adrian lay dying at a Bay Area hospital. I drove over to he with them.

Adrian's hospital room was filled with family, relatives and hospital staff. He had been an outgoing youngster with a zest for life that brought joy to all who knew him. Eddie, his father, explained that Adrian had been in a coma for thirteen hours. Each breath was accompanied by a spasm that shook his entire body.

"I wish he could just let go," Eddie said tearfully. We walked outside to talk and Eddie explained how his son's suffering had brought him to the point where his only wish was for Adrian to he out of his pain.

For years Eddie had urged Adrian to be strong in his fight for life. Adrian had responded, and had far outlived his prognosis. But now Adrian's fighting on was only prolonging suffering.

I asked Eddie if he had told Adrian that it was all right to let go now. I knew Adrian worshipped his father and would never want to let him down,

"Maybe Adrian thinks he's failing you if he dies. Maybe that's why he keeps fighting so hard.

Eddie burst into tears. "But I want him to stop fighting now," he said. "He's been such a good boy, and fought hard enough."

At that moment I recalled a Native American elder who years ago taught me the difference between quitting, versus surrendering, or giving over to something higher than yourself. I told Eddie of this differentiation, and that maybe it would be helpful to Adrian. Adrian wasn't giving up or quitting. He'd fought courageously and could now release victoriously into the heaven he'd dreamed about the night before he had slipped into the coma.

Eddie responded with enthusiasm. He was proud of his son, and while saddened and already mourning his loss, wanted Adrian to go on now to the release he so desperately needed and deserved. Eddie believed that even though Adrian was in a coma, we could still communicate with him through the love in our hearts, and that he would hear us.

We walked back to the room and told the doctor of our plan. He agreed with us on the need to let Adrian know he hadn't failed anyone, and could now let go, with his family's blessings, into a higher state of being that he had justly earned. Eddie, the doctor and I re-entered the jammed hospital room. We silently extended our "release message." I focused all my attention on supporting

24

Adrian in knowing it was okay to let go.

Time wore on and still he struggled. To my dismay, I began to get frustrated because Adrian was not letting go.

Then I realized that it was I who needed to let go. I was holding on to having Adrian die on my timing, to meet my agenda. Adrian had his own timing that needed to he respected. My role as a "birther" was not to project my needs and timing onto his, thereby interfering with whatever he might he dealing with in the mystery of his "doing" his dying. I had to refocus on extending my love to him unconditionally, and release him into his own experience. Slowly I realized that Adrian was teaching me the importance of really letting go, cleanly and with clarity with love that wanted nothing in return.

I smiled inside, and thanked him for his gift. Adrian died shortly thereafter. I could almost hear him chuckle a congratulatory "I'm glad you finally got the message Tom," as the last breath left his body.

Richard Boerstler, a modern death education specialist, asks a relevant question to situations such as the one with Adrian, "If your own mind is destined to become the universe itself, what state of consciousness do you wish to be in at the moment of passage?" My experience with Adrian raises an additional question. "What state of consciousness do you wish those around you to be in as you move through your dying process?"

The teachers I have been fortunate to experience all point to an open heart and an enlightened mind, i.e. a mind filled with light and free of all baggage save the quality of light, as being the best qualities for the birthing process we call death. How do we develop these qualities? Can we learn them, and must we wait for our own death for the spiritualization of consciousness they foster to occur?

"No," answers Dr. Salvadore Roquet, a Mexican psychiatrist who utilizes shamanistic ritual and rites of passage in his innovative work with patients. "We need to face death to come to life and live it, which is to love." He asserts that we need to deal with the fears that keep us from living and loving. We need to acknowledge and use them in a positive way, for they can sink or launch us. Roquet believes there is potentiality for spiritual realization inherent within all human beings.

"It is only a thing of liberating it, of freeing it from our subconscious, he says. We have only to let it out and see it." In our fears about death and our attempts in "not dying, we die," he states, because "we imprison ourselves in fear and weaken our capacities to live full, creatively productive, and loving lives."

An old shamanistic practice is cultivating the ability to turn your head and look into the face of your own, inevitable death, and to know that, given the right timing, you will enter its embrace. The goal isn't to encourage despair and sadness. Instead it is to activate an awareness that this very moment is all you have. Face the truth that the act you are doing now may he your last one, so do it well with full consciousness. In facing the reality of death in such a manner, we come full circle back into life again. Only now we can live it with a fullness and vitality that wasn't possible when we did not face our fears directly.

Facing death directly brings forth a sense of humility. Yesterday I spent several hours with a middle-aged man prior to his undergoing major surgery. He had a vague abstract belief in God, but had been living his life based on his own gratification with little regard for others. He had been impressed with his own power to achieve these ends. But now fearful that he might die in surgery, of which there was a good chance, he suddenly saw how small his power really was, and the myopic vision that had characterized his previous activity.

Modern western society, with its emphasis on technological prowess and material riches, has become impoverished in spiritual riches, which are the only ones that count when death comes to call. Aboriginal rites of passage provide opportunity to practice the art of releasing into the great unknown. This in turn can strengthen the development of humility and other spiritual riches such as patience, trust and the ability to he open, honest and present in the moment.

In the seeking of vision from the Great Spirit for guidance in one's life path, Native American youths were instructed in the importance of a humble attitude. Sacred knowledge, they learned, cannot he attained while arrogant and prideful. You cannot pour water into an already filled pitcher-all you get is a mess.

To open to the luminous state of our deeper being requires humility. Black Elk, a Lakota Sioux medicine man, teaches that unless one humbles oneself before the entire creation, before even the smallest ant, one cannot gain peace.

Peace comes only from seeing and knowing our relationship

and oneness with the universe and all its powers, and realizing that at its center dwells Wakan Tanka (translated as Sacred Mystery) and that this center is within each of us.

"Only in being nothing may man become everything," he says, "and only then does he realize his essential brotherhood with all forms of Life." Without this expanded vision and recognition of the sacredness of human-kind's deeper being, we get lost in the darkness of ego.

The youth questing for vision had further training and inculcation of humility in the purifying rites of the Sweatlodge Ceremony preceding the Quest. The sweatlodge is somewhat physically similar to a steam-bath. You go inside and sweat. But the sweatlodge had symbolic significance with every aspect of its construction and spiritual purpose through the acts of prayer and ceremony that take place within it. Death preparation is evident in Black Elk's explanation of the willow branches used in its framing. "These too have a lesson to teach us, for in the fall their leaves die and return to the earth, but in the spring they come to life again. So too, men die but live again in the real world of Wakan Tanka, where there is nothing but the spirits of all things. This true life we may know here on earth if we purify our bodies and minds, thus coming closer to Wakan Tanka who is all purity. Thus we may see not only with our two eyes, but with the one eye which is of the heart, and with which we see and know all that is true and good."

Experiences such as the Sweatlodge Ceremony and the vision quest emphasized the importance of self-discipline, concentration, patience, focused will and intent. These in turn encouraged listening to the gifts of the looks within place, or inner attunement, as a source of knowledge. These qualities were instrumental in the positive utilization of altered states of consciousness precipitated by these rites wherein the Native American people sought spiritual renewal. The expanded consciousness provided opportunity to explore levels of reality beyond the observable world of sensory-based perception and ego control. Through the temporary loss of the structured self into a larger realm of the transpersonal, participants could experience the phenomena of ego-death. This same phenomena has been reported by clinical researchers using psychoactive drugs with terminally ill patients. Some reports of near-death experience also describe the dissolving of ego into an expanded state. People who experience temporary ego-death, through rites of passage, or a near-death experience, enhance their ability to surrender control into the mysterious unknown with faith and trust. Greater familiarity and knowledge with a level of existence deeper, broader and richer than the one known in our normative state of consciousness, brings forth more confidence with the idea of total release into it at the time of physical death.

All the great religions of the world attest to Epes Brown's statement that, "there is no greater error to which man is subject than to believe that his real self is nothing more than his own body or mind." The impact of this error of perception and identity manifests with full force when death approaches, especially if it has not been previously addressed. How the dying person and those around them respond to it, as Virginia Hine reminds us, helps determine the quality of the death experience. A story of a death with quality and the life-teachings it holds concludes this writing "assignment."

Tommy was a dynamic youth of fourteen years of age who lay dying of leukemia. His father, whom I knew from the Parent's Group at the Center, called to tell me of Tommy's condition, He called back shortly thereafter to describe the transformational teaching his son gave him in his final passage.

Tommy was in and out of a coma the last few hours of his life. His death myth involved a belief in an afterlife that included a journey to Hawaii. I had given Tommy some coral I'd obtained on a dive trip to Hawaii when I visited him in the hospital several days earlier. His father told me later that Tommy kept it by his bedside throughout his hospital stay. Tommy was concerned that when he died he wouldn't know how to get there, and this was a major worry for him.

Tommy was in an altered state as he approached death. He reported seeing two butterflies moving in the room. Then he asked his mother if she knew how to meditate. When she said no, Tommy had her, his stepmother and his father sit next to one another in a circle on his bed. He had them all join hands together. His father then described feeling a burst of light come out of Tommy and go around the circle, "It was a circle of love," he said. "It had no beginning and it had no end. When Tommy had that love going just right, because that's what he wanted to teach us about, then he stepped out."

Tommy's father then described seeing the now healthy image

of his son emerge from the emaciated body lying on the bed. Two hands held his son's hands. They were the guides to help Tommy on his journey, two friends who had just recently died of cancer themselves. Together the three boys rose up above the bed. Tommy had his long blond hair back that had been lost with the chemotherapy treatments. He shook his head, smiled and rose on up and out of the room. Tommy's father explained somewhat sheepishly that he hadn't really seen this occur with his eyes. He saw it, he said, with his heart.

Tommy's passage over the threshold of death initiated his father into an expanded level of awareness with a deeper way of knowing than that to which he was accustomed. The circle without beginning or end, available to us all whenever we open our hearts to touch and be touched, and to give freely of the love within, unites us as one. It is a birthing of a fuller and richer state of being, one that empowers our experience of now wherever we find ourselves on the great universal wheel of life and death.

When Tommy's father spoke with embarrassment of his heart vision, I told him of psychiatrist Carl Jung's experience in the American southwest described in Memories, Dreams and Reflections. A Pueblo elder confided to Jung that he thought all white people were mad. When Jung questioned him on statement, he replied that white people were mad because they thought with their heads.

"What do you think with?" asked Jung in surprise. The elder's response provides guidance for truly honoring the sacred birthing potential inherent in the experience of death. It applies equally to the person undergoing the passage, their loved ones in attendance, and the helping professional.

The old man raised his hand silently pointed to the middle of his chest. "We think here," he, said, indicating his heart.

AFTERWORD

It has been many years since I had the experiences that led to writing *"Do They Celebrate Christmas in Heaven?"* The passage of time illuminates even brighter the lessons they taught me.

Their quality of truth provides strength and courage to "keep on keeping on" with trust and faith in the ever present power of love It's not always easy. Sometimes I get stuck in darkness, either my own, or what I see around me, Then I remember Tommy's Circle of Love, and that it has no beginning and no end. It's here, right now, present always, with whomever and wherever you or I find ourselves. The key to entering the circle to know its full richness is really very simple.

"We need only to open our hearts to the presence of unconditional love and remember that we are sacred, worthy, luminous beings, and we are love and our love is for giving.

About the Author

Tom Pinkson was born in the heart of New York City in 1945. The death of his father when he was four years old set him on path of exploration that began with psychosomatic illness, and later juvenile delinquency, but eventually took him to the far reaches of the Amazon jungle, the Andes mountains and to an eleven year apprenticeship with a group of Huichol Indian shaman in the Sierra Madre of north central Mexico. Seeking deeper truth about the mysteries of life and death, he sought out and found numerous shamanic "Medicine" Teachers who initiated him into totally different realms than those from which he had come.

During this time Tom also earned three college degrees, including a Ph.D. in psychology. His doctoral dissertation, *"A Quest for Vision,"* described his successful work with heroin addicts in the early 1970s using a wilderness treatment program that included mountain climbing, river running, snow camping, ski touring and vision quests in the High Sierra. The quests continue to this day, forty years later with people coming from all over the United States to join him on these powerful experiences of solitude and adventure in the back country of Yosemite. From working with drug addicts, he went on to help start the second hospice programs in the United States, offering support services to the terminally ill. From there, he was invited to join Dr. Jerry Jampolsky at the Center for Attitudinal Healing in Tiburon California to work with children facing life-threatening illness.

Tom went on to create his *"Recognition Rites for a New Vision of Aging Honoring Elders Program"*, along with recording a CD of fourteen of his "message songs" using music and song to open hearts and minds to the wisdom of deep being. Walking in two worlds, the shamanic world of indigenous spirituality, and the Western world of a psychologist, consultant, teacher, public speaker, sacred story-teller, ceremonial and retreat leader and performance artist, Tom serves as a bridge-builder, bringing what he calls *"The Teachings of the Elders"* into practical applications within the modern, urban setting. From major corporations to pediatric oncology units within prestigious cancer treatment centers, from the academic world to rites of passage work with children, adolescents and adults, the dying process and subsequent work of grief, mourning, and rebirth, Tom has successfully brought in wisdom teachings from the *"Elders"* that have had dramatic impact in enriching people's lives.

He is an internationally published author and the founder and president of a nonprofit, spiritually-based educational community, Wakan, which offers a variety of programs and services helping people find and remember what is sacred in their lives. He has Tom has two grown children, three grandchildren and lives with his wisdom-woman wife Andrea, in San Anselmo, California..

CONTACT INFORMATION

To learn more about Tom's work, please visit his websites: www.drtompinkson.com and www.nierica.com. You can contact him via email at: tompinkson@gmail.com.